Baking with Fruit

Baking with Fruit

Delicious cakes, pastries, and desserts

This edition published by Parragon Books Ltd in 2013 and distributed by
Parragon Inc.
440 Park Avenue South, 13th Floor
New York, NY 10016
www.parragon.com/lovefood

LOVE FOOD is an imprint of Parragon Books Ltd

ISBN 978-1-4723-2975-2

Printed in China

Recipes, photographs, and food styling: Patrik Jaros / www.food-experts-group.com
Edited by: Sabine Vonderstein & Patrik Jaros
Lace: from the book *Lace*, by The Pepin Press, www.pepinpress.com

Notes for the Reader

This book uses standard kitchen measuring spoons and cups. All spoon and cup measurements are level unless otherwise indicated. Unless otherwise stated, milk is assumed to be whole and eggs are large.

Garnishes, decorations, and serving suggestions are all optional and not necessarily included in the recipe ingredients or method.

The times given are only an approximate guide. Preparation times differ according to the techniques used by different people and the cooking times may also vary from those given. Optional ingredients, variations, or serving suggestions have not been included in the time calculations.

Recipes using raw or very lightly cooked eggs should be avoided by infants, the elderly, pregnant women, convalescents, and anyone with a weakened immune system. Pregnant and breast-feeding women are advised to avoid eating peanuts and peanut products. People with nut allergies should be aware that some of the prepared ingredients used in the recipes in this book may contain nuts. Always check the packaging before use.

Contents

Foreword

Fresh, sweet, and juicy fruit of almost every variety can be used in tempting baked treats of all shapes and forms. Family cakes, flans, tarts, pastries, desserts, and sheet cakes can all incorporate the sensory pleasures of fruit from the garden or the market. Nowadays, most kinds of fruit are available to be enjoyed all year round, but it makes sense to pay attention to the seasons when choosing which cake to bake. Rhubarb, for example, is only available in the spring, while plums taste best when they are at their ripest in late summer.

The authors have reinterpreted traditional and well-known recipes, as well as having created some exciting new flavor combinations, to produce a collection of more than 40 delicious cakes and baked goods using fresh fruit. From delectable little tarts to refreshing fruit flans, this book provides a wealth of ideas for inspiration. Whether it's for a cozy afternoon get-together over coffee and cake, a Sunday visit from relatives or a fun-packed children's birthday, there's a fruity treat to suit every taste and every occasion.

Let yourself be tempted by traditional cakes, such as Grandma's Cherry Cake or Lemon Sponge Roll; unusual combinations, such as Pomegranate Cheesecake or Fig and Orange Liqueur Cake; or modern creations, such as Banana and Chocolate Flan or Chilled Buttermilk and Kiwi Flan. There are beautiful photographs of all the cakes; bound to encourage you to try making them yourself, and at the same time also giving you some presentation ideas. Don't be discouraged if not every cake you bake turns out looking just like the picture the first time—at least you can be sure it will taste good.

Happy baking!

Fruit for every
season ...

Rhubarb Cake

Makes one 12 × 16-inch cake

Preparation time: 45 minutes
Cooking time: 45 minutes

Cake
2 tablespoons dried bread crumbs
3¼ cups all-purpose flour
2 teaspoons baking powder
2¼ sticks butter, plus extra for greasing
⅔ cup granulated sugar
4 eggs
pinch of salt
½ cup milk

Topping
16 rhubarb stalks (about 1¾ pounds), trimmed
¼ cup granulated sugar
1 teaspoon vanilla sugar or a few drops vanilla extract
confectioners' sugar, for dusting

1 Preheat the oven to 350°F. Grease a shallow 12 x 16-inch baking pan and sprinkle with the bread crumbs.

2 To make the cake, mix together the flour and baking powder. Put the butter into a large bowl and beat with an electric mixer until fluffy, then gradually add the sugar, eggs, salt, and flour mixture, beating after each addition until combined.

3 Add the milk, a little at a time, beating until smooth. Spoon the batter into the prepared pan and level the surface with a spatula.

4 To make the topping, cut the rhubarb into ¾-inch lengths. Mix with the granulated sugar and vanilla sugar or vanilla extract.

5 Spread the rhubarb pieces evenly over the batter. Bake in the preheated oven for about 45 minutes. Remove from the oven, let cool, and dust with confectioners' sugar before serving. Best served lukewarm with whipped cream or vanilla ice cream.

Tip: To make vanilla sugar, put a vanilla bean, cut lengthwise, into a jar of granulated sugar and set aside for at least a week, until needed.

Strawberry and Lemon Tart

Makes one 11-inch tart

Preparation time: 55 minutes, plus 30 minutes to chill
Cooking time: 1 hour 10 minutes

Pastry dough
1⅓ cups all-purpose flour, plus extra for dusting
1 egg
5½ tablespoons butter
2½ tablespoons granulated sugar
pinch of salt

Filling
¾ cup milk
1 cup heavy cream
3 tablespoons confectioners' sugar
grated rind of 2 lemons
4 egg yolks

Topping
1 cup black currants or blueberries
⅓ cup confectioners' sugar
1¼ pounds ripe small strawberries, hulled
grated rind of 1 small lemon, for sprinkling

1 To make the pastry dough, mix together the flour, egg, butter, sugar, and salt in a mixing bowl, then knead by hand until a smooth dough forms. Wrap the dough in plastic wrap and chill in the refrigerator for at least 30 minutes.

2 Meanwhile, to make the filling, put the milk into a saucepan with the cream, confectioners' sugar, and lemon rind. Bring to a boil, remove from the heat, then let steep for 30 minutes. Gently beat the egg yolks into the lemon cream.

3 Preheat the oven to 350°F. Line an 11-inch round, fluted tart pan with parchment paper.

4 Roll out the dough on a work surface lightly dusted with flour to a 12-inch circle. Use to line the prepared pan, trimming off any excess with a sharp knife. Prick the bottom with a fork in several places.

5 Line the dough with parchment paper, then fill with pie weights or dried beans and bake on the bottom shelf of the preheated oven for 15 minutes. Remove the paper and weights and bake for an additional 15 minutes, then remove from the oven and reduce the oven temperature to 275°F. Pour the warm egg mixture into the pastry shell and return to the oven for about 40 minutes, until set. Remove from the oven and let cool completely.

6 To make the topping, thoroughly mash the black currants and mix them with the confectioners' sugar, then pass the mixture through a fine strainer to make a puree.

7 Top the tart with a tightly packed layer of strawberries, then drizzle with the black currant puree and sprinkle with lemon rind.

Strawberry Tarts with Vanilla Crème

Makes four 4-inch tarts

Preparation time: 40 minutes,
plus 30 minutes to chill
Cooking time: 18 minutes

Sponge
butter, for greasing
2 eggs, separated
½ cup granulated sugar
1 tablespoon vanilla sugar (see page 10) or a few drops vanilla extract
pinch of salt
⅓ cup all-purpose flour, plus extra for dusting
⅓ cup cornstarch

Vanilla crème
2 eggs, separated
1 envelope vanilla pudding and pie filling mix
1½ cups milk
⅔ cup heavy cream
⅓ cup granulated sugar
1 teaspoon vanilla sugar or a few drops vanilla extract

Topping
2 tablespoons slivered almonds
confectioners' sugar, for toasting and dusting
1¼ pounds strawberries, hulled

1 Preheat the oven to 400°F. Grease four 4-inch round tart pans and dust with flour.

2 To make the sponge, put the egg yolks into a bowl and beat with an electric mixer until fluffy, adding the granulated sugar and vanilla sugar or vanilla extract a little at a time. In a separate bowl, beat the egg whites with the salt until they hold stiff peaks. Mix the flour with the cornstarch and fold into the egg yolk mixture with the egg whites.

3 Divide the batter among the prepared pans and level the surface with a spatula. Bake on the bottom shelf of the preheated oven for about 18 minutes, until golden brown. Let cool slightly, then turn out onto a wire rack to cool completely.

4 To make the vanilla crème, blend the egg yolks with the pudding and pie filling mix and ¼ cup of the milk. Put the remaining milk into a saucepan, add the cream, granulated sugar, and vanilla sugar or vanilla extract, and bring to a boil. Pour in the pudding mixture and bring to a boil, stirring continuously, then remove from the heat. Pour the crème into a bowl, cover with plastic wrap, and chill in the refrigerator for 30 minutes. Remove from the refrigerator and whisk vigorously with a wire whisk.

5 To make the topping, toast the slivered almonds with a little confectioners' sugar in a dry skillet until golden brown.

6 Spread the vanilla crème on top of the sponge cakes. Place the strawberries on top with their points facing upward. Sprinkle the almonds over the tarts and dust with confectioners' sugar.

Tip: Also tastes great with any other berries of your choice.

Fruits of the Forest Cheesecake

Makes one 9½-inch cake

Preparation time: 20 minutes, plus 4½ hours to chill

Crust
9 ounces graham crackers or plain cookies
1 stick butter
⅓ cup granulated sugar
pinch of ground cinnamon

Topping
3 egg yolks
½ cup granulated sugar
2 cups mascarpone cheese
4 cups mixed berries, such as raspberries, blackberries, and blueberries
12 sheets gelatin
1 cup heavy cream
3 ounces small, light cookies
confectioners' sugar, for dusting

1 To make the crust, put the graham crackers or plain cookies into a plastic bag and crush with a rolling pin until reduced to fine crumbs. Melt the butter in a saucepan, add the crumbs, sugar, and cinnamon, and mix to combine. Line the bottom of a 9½-inch round springform pan with parchment paper, press the crumb mixture into the bottom, then chill in the refrigerator for 30 minutes.

2 To make the topping, put the egg yolks into a large bowl with the sugar and beat with an electric mixer until fluffy. Add the mascarpone cheese and 2½ cups of the berries. Soak the gelatin in cold water for 10 minutes, then squeeze out the water. Put the gelatin into a saucepan with a little water and heat over low heat, stirring continuously, until dissolved. Stir the gelatin into the mascarpone mixture.

3 Whip the cream until it holds stiff peaks and fold it into the mascarpone mixture. Spread the mixture on the bottom, cover with plastic wrap, and chill in the refrigerator for 4 hours.

4 Remove the cake from the refrigerator and decorate with the remaining berries. Unclip and release the springform, arrange the small cookies around the edge of the cake, and dust with confectioners' sugar.

Mini Charlotte Russes

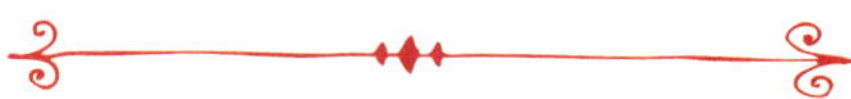

Makes eight mini charlottes

Preparation time: 40 minutes, plus 2 hours to chill
Cooking time: 12 minutes

Crème
5 sheets gelatin
½ vanilla bean
1 cup milk
2 ounces white chocolate, broken into small pieces
3 egg yolks
3 tablespoons granulated sugar
1 cup heavy cream

Ladyfingers
3 eggs, separated
⅓ cup confectioners' sugar
1 teaspoon vanilla sugar (see page 10) or a few drops vanilla extract
pinch of salt
¼ cup granulated sugar, plus extra for sprinkling
½ cup all-purpose flour, sifted
¼ cup cornstarch

To decorate
1 cup raspberries
1 cup blueberries
confectioners' sugar, for dusting

1 To make the crème, soak the gelatin in cold water for 10 minutes. Meanwhile, halve the vanilla bean lengthwise and scrape out the seeds. Put the milk into a small saucepan, add the vanilla seeds, and bring to a boil. Add the chocolate and let melt.

2 Put the egg yolks and granulated sugar into a heatproof bowl and beat with an electric mixer until fluffy, then slowly stir in the hot milk. Set the bowl over a saucepan of gently simmering water and beat the crème until it thickens. (Alternatively, use a double boiler.) Remove from the heat. Squeeze the water out of the gelatin, add the gelatin to the mixture, and stir to dissolve. Pass through a fine strainer into a bowl. Transfer to the refrigerator to cool.

3 Whip the cream until it holds stiff peaks. Fold half the cream into the crème, then whisk in the remainder with a wire whisk. Divide the batter among eight deep ½-cup molds, cover with plastic wrap, and chill in the refrigerator for 2 hours until set.

4 Preheat the oven to 350°F. Line a baking sheet with parchment paper. To make the ladyfingers, put the egg yolks into a bowl with the confectioners' sugar and vanilla sugar or vanilla extract, and beat until fluffy. Beat the egg whites with the salt and granulated sugar until they hold stiff peaks. Fold the egg whites into the egg yolk mixture, then fold in the flour and cornstarch.

5 Put the batter in a pastry bag fitted with a ⅜-inch tip, and pipe the batter onto the prepared baking sheet in 2-inch lengths. Sprinkle with granulated sugar and bake in the preheated oven for about 12 minutes. Remove from the oven and let cool.

6 Loosen the edges of the charlottes with a knife and turn them out of the molds. Arrange the ladyfingers around the edges, decorate the tops with the fruit, dust with confectioners' sugar, and serve.

Berry and Sparkling Wine Gelatin with Crème Fraîche

Makes one 2½-cup gelatin

Preparation time: 25 minutes, plus 6 hours to set

12 sheets gelatin
3 cups dry white sparkling wine
⅓ cup granulated sugar
1 teaspoon vanilla sugar (see page 10) or a few drops vanilla extract
1⅓ cups halved, hulled strawberries
1 cup blackberries
1 cup blueberries
1 cup black currants (or extra blueberries)
1 cup raspberries
1 cup crème fraîche or Greek yogurt
1 teaspoon confectioners' sugar

1 Soak the gelatin sheets in cold water for about 10 minutes.

2 Meanwhile, put ½ cup of the wine into a saucepan with the granulated sugar and vanilla sugar or vanilla extract and heat over low heat. Squeeze out the gelatin and add it to the wine, stirring to dissolve. Pour into a bowl and add the remaining wine. As soon as the gelatin starts to set, add all the berries, then pour into a 2½-cup glass mold. Cover with plastic wrap and chill in the refrigerator for about 6 hours, until set.

3 Dip the mold briefly into a bowl of warm water to loosen the gelatin. Turn out the gelatin onto a serving plate.

4 Just before serving, mix the crème fraîche or Greek yogurt with the confectioners' sugar and drizzle it over the gelatin.

Berry Tarts with Butter Crumb Topping

Makes six 4-inch tarts

Preparation time: 25 minutes, plus 30 minutes to chill
Cooking time: 35 minutes

Pastry dough
1¼ cups all-purpose flour
1 teaspoon baking powder
1 stick butter, plus extra for greasing
¾ cup granulated sugar
1 teaspoon vanilla sugar (see page 10) or a few drops vanilla extract
pinch of salt
1 egg

Crumb topping
¾ cup all-purpose flour
½ cup ground almonds (almond meal)
½ cup granulated sugar
1 teaspoon vanilla sugar
1 stick butter, softened

Filling
2 cups raspberries
1 cup blueberries
1 cup blackberries
confectioners' sugar, for dusting

1 Preheat the oven to 350°F. Grease six 4-inch round tart pans.

2 To make the pastry dough, mix together the flour and the baking powder in a mixing bowl. Cut the butter into small pieces, rub into the flour mixture, then add the granulated sugar, vanilla sugar or vanilla extract, salt, and egg, and knead until a firm dough forms. Roll the dough into a ball, wrap with plastic wrap, and chill in the refrigerator for about 30 minutes.

3 Divide the dough into six pieces and press one piece into each of the prepared pans. Bake in the preheated oven for 15 minutes, then remove from the oven and let cool in the pans. Do not turn off the oven.

4 To make the crumb topping, put all the ingredients into a bowl and rub together with your fingertips until a crumbly texture is achieved.

5 To make the filling, sprinkle the berries over the pastry shells and sprinkle with the crumb topping.

6 Bake the tarts in the oven for 20 minutes, then let cool in the pans. Release them from the pans using the point of a knife, dust with confectioners' sugar, and serve.

Blueberry Crisp with Walnuts

Makes one 10-inch crisp

Preparation time: 30 minutes, plus 30 minutes to chill
Cooking time: 35 minutes

Crust
2 cups all-purpose flour, plus extra for dusting
1 teaspoon baking powder
⅓ cup granulated sugar
1 teaspoon vanilla sugar (see page 10) or a few drops vanilla extract
1 stick butter, plus extra for greasing
2 eggs
2 tablespoons dried bread crumbs

Filling
3 cups blueberries
2 egg yolks
½ cup granulated sugar
1 tablespoon vanilla sugar or a few drops vanilla extract
3 tablespoons milk
1 cup ground walnuts
1 cup all-purpose flour
confectioners' sugar, for dusting

1 To make the crust, mix together the flour, baking powder, granulated sugar, and vanilla sugar or vanilla extract. Cut the butter into small pieces, rub into the flour mixture, then add the eggs. Quickly knead the mixture until a smooth dough forms. Wrap in plastic wrap and chill in the refrigerator for at least 30 minutes.

2 Preheat the oven to 325°F. Grease a 10-inch round tart pan.

3 Roll out the dough on a work surface lightly dusted with flour into a circle slightly larger than the prepared pan. Use it to line the pan, turning up the edge of the dough. Prick the bottom several times with a fork and sprinkle with the bread crumbs.

4 To make the filling, spread the blueberries over the dough. Mix the egg yolks with the granulated sugar, vanilla sugar or vanilla extract, and milk. Add the walnuts and flour and rub together with your fingertips until a crumbly texture is achieved. Sprinkle the crumb mixture over the blueberries.

5 Bake in the preheated oven for about 35 minutes, until the crumb is light brown. Let cool slightly, then dust with confectioners' sugar just before serving.

Walnut Sponge Roll with Pear Filling

Makes one 16-inch roll

Preparation time: 45 minutes, plus 5 hours to cool
Cooking time: 20 minutes

Sponge
4 eggs
¼ cup lukewarm water
¼ cup granulated sugar
⅔ cup all-purpose flour
⅓ cup cornstarch
½ cup ground walnuts
1 teaspoon baking powder

Filling
4–5 Bosc pears (about 1¾ pounds)
1¾ cups pear juice
juice of ½ lemon
pinch of ground cinnamon
⅓ cup granulated sugar
4 sheets gelatin
1 cup heavy cream
confectioners' sugar, for dusting

1 Preheat the oven to 325°F. Line a shallow 12 x 16-inch baking pan with parchment paper.

2 To make the sponge, separate the eggs. Put the egg whites into a bowl with the water and beat with an electric mixer until they hold stiff peaks. Slowly stir in the sugar, then carefully fold in the egg yolks. Mix together the flour, cornstarch, walnuts, and baking powder in a separate bowl, then carefully fold the flour mixture into the egg mixture.

3 Spread the batter evenly in the prepared pan and bake in the middle of the preheated oven for about 20 minutes.

4 Remove from the oven and turn out the pan onto a damp dish towel. Brush the parchment paper with cold water and quickly peel it off the sponge. Use the dish towel to roll up the sponge from the long side, then let cool for 2 hours.

5 To make the filling, peel, core, and slice the pears. Put the pear slices in a saucepan with the pear juice, lemon juice, cinnamon, and sugar, bring to a boil, then remove from the heat. Soak the gelatin sheets in a little water, then squeeze out the water and stir the gelatin into the warm pear syrup and let cool.

6 Whip the cream until it holds stiff peaks. As soon as the pear mixture starts to set, gently fold in the cream.

7 Carefully unroll the sponge and spread the filling over it. Roll up again immediately and let cool for an additional 3 hours. Dust with confectioners' sugar just before serving.

Pear and Blackberry Cake

Makes one 12 × 16-inch cake

Preparation time: 1 hour 15 minutes, plus 1 hour to rise
Cooking time: 30 minutes

Cake
4 cups all-purpose flour, plus extra for dusting
¼ cup granulated sugar
pinch of salt
1 tablespoon active dry yeast (1½ envelopes)
1 stick butter, plus extra for greasing
1¼ cups lukewarm milk

Topping
3 Bosc pears
rind of 1 orange
2 cups blackberries
¼ cup firmly packed light brown sugar
⅓ cup quince jelly or apricot preserves
confectioners' sugar, for dusting

1 To make the cake, sift the flour, sugar, and salt into a large bowl then stir in the yeast. Make a well in the center.

2 Melt the butter in a saucepan over low heat, then add to the dry ingredients with the milk, mixing to a soft, smooth dough. Cover with a damp dish towel and let rise in a warm place for about 30 minutes, or until risen and springy to the touch.

3 Meanwhile, grease a 12 x 16-inch baking pan. To make the topping, peel, quarter, and core the pears, then cut the quarters into slices. Cut the orange rind into narrow strips.

4 Roll out the dough on a work surface lightly dusted with flour to a rectangle the size of the prepared pan. Lay the dough in the pan. Arrange the pears, blackberries, and strips of orange rind evenly on top, pressing them into the dough slightly, then sprinkle with the brown sugar. Let rise for 30 minutes.

5 Meanwhile, preheat the oven to 400°F.

6 Bake the cake in the preheated oven for about 30 minutes. Put the quince jelly into a small saucepan and heat over low heat. Brush the jelly on the warm cake and let cool. Dust with confectioners' sugar just before serving.

Blackberry and Semolina Cake

Makes one 8½-inch cake

Preparation time: 30 minutes
Cooking time: 1 hour

Cake
1 stick butter
¾ cup granulated sugar
3 eggs
grated rind and juice of 1 orange
⅔ cup semolina flour
1 teaspoon baking powder
1 envelope vanilla pudding and pie filling mix
2 cups low-fat fromage blanc, mascarpone, or ricotta cheese

Topping
3½ cups blackberries
½ cup confectioners' sugar, plus extra for dusting

1 Preheat the oven to 350°F. Line an 8½-inch round springform pan with parchment paper.

2 To make the cake, put the butter into a bowl and beat with an electric mixer until fluffy. Add the sugar, eggs, and orange rind and juice and beat until smooth.

3 Mix the semolina flour with the baking powder and pudding and pie filling mix. Stir into the butter mixture, then add the fromage blanc, mascarpone, or ricotta cheese and mix to combine.

4 Spoon the mixture into the prepared pan and level the surface. Bake in the preheated oven for about 60 minutes, until golden brown.

5 Let the cake cool in the pan for 1–2 minutes, then unclip and release the springform and transfer the cake to a wire rack. Peel off the parchment paper and let the cake cool completely.

6 To make the topping, crush 1 cup of the blackberries with the confectioners' sugar and pass through a fine strainer. Heap the remaining blackberries on top of the cake, pour over the strained blackberries, and dust with confectioners' sugar just before serving.

Tip: Instead of semolina, the cake can also be made with fine cornmeal, which gives it a wonderful yellow color. Strawberries or blueberries can also be used for the topping.

Meringue and Puff Pastry Slices with Berries

Makes eight slices

Preparation time: 30 minutes
Cooking time: 15 minutes

6 sheets ready-to-bake puff pastry
all-purpose flour, for dusting
1 egg yolk, beaten
⅓ cup slivered almonds
1 cup heavy cream
⅔ cup superfine sugar or granulated sugar
2 egg whites
1 vanilla bean, halved lengthwise and seeds removed
1 cup blueberries
1 cup raspberries
1⅓ cups red currants or other berries of your choice
confectioners' sugar, for dusting

1 Preheat the oven to 375°F. Line a shallow 2 x 16-inch baking pan with parchment paper.

2 Divide the pastry into two piles, using three sheets in each, dust with flour, and roll out to a thickness of about ½ inch. Lay the pastry on the prepared pan.

3 Brush the two slabs of pastry with the beaten egg yolk. Sprinkle with the almonds and bake on the bottom shelf of the preheated oven for about 15 minutes, until golden brown. Remove from the oven and let cool.

4 Whip the cream with 2 tablespoons of the superfine or granulated sugar until it holds stiff peaks. Cover and chill in the refrigerator until required. Beat the egg whites until they hold soft peaks, beat in the remaining sugar, a little at a time, then add the vanilla seeds. Beat until the egg white is glossy and holds stiff peaks. Fold in the whipped cream.

5 Split each piece of pastry in half horizontally. Spread the bottom halves with half of the meringue mixture, sprinkle the berries on top, and spread the remaining meringue mixture on top of the berries. Top with the remaining pastry halves. Dust with confectioners' sugar just before serving and cut each piece into four slices.

Tip: The puff pastry slices can also be filled with a vanilla crème (see page 14), and other fruits can be used.

Lime and Raspberry Tart

Makes one 9½-inch tart

Preparation time: 45 minutes, plus 1 hour to chill
Cooking time: 1 hour 5 minutes

Pastry dough
1⅓ cups all-purpose flour, plus extra for dusting
1 egg
6 tablespoons butter
2½ tablespoons granulated sugar
½ teaspoon salt

Filling
1 cup milk
1 cup heavy cream
1 cup confectioners' sugar
rind of 2 limes, in long strips
6 egg yolks
4 cups raspberries (about 1¼ pounds)

Crème
1 cup mascarpone cheese
⅔ cup confectioners' sugar, plus extra for dusting
grated rind and juice of 1 lime
grated lime rind, to decorate (optional)

1 To make the pastry dough, put the flour, egg, butter, sugar, and salt into a food processor and process to a smooth dough. Shape into a ball, wrap in plastic wrap, and chill in the refrigerator for about 30 minutes.

2 To make the filling, put the milk, cream, sugar, and lime rind into a saucepan and bring to a boil, then remove from the heat and let steep for 30 minutes. Remove the lime rind from the cream mixture and carefully beat in the egg yolks.

3 Line the bottom of a 9½-inch round tart pan with parchment paper. Roll out the dough on a work surface lightly dusted with flour into a 12-inch circle. Place it in the prepared pan, pressing it into the side of the pan and trimming any excess. Prick the bottom with a fork in several places, dust with a little flour, and chill for 30 minutes.

4 Preheat the oven to 350°F. Line the pastry shell with parchment paper, fill with pie weights or dried beans, and bake on the bottom shelf of the preheated oven for 15 minutes. Remove the paper and weights and bake for an additional 15 minutes. Remove from the oven and reduce the oven temperature to 275°F. Heat the egg mixture briefly, then pour it into pastry shell, reserving 2 tablespoons, and bake for 35 minutes. Remove from the oven and let cool.

5 Arrange the raspberries on top of the tart.

6 To make the crème, beat the mascarpone cheese with the reserved egg mixture, the confectioners' sugar, and the lime rind and juice until smooth. Pour into the middle of the tart, leaving a border around the edge where the raspberries are still visible. Dust with confectioners' sugar, sprinkle some grated lime rind on top, if using, and serve.

Red Currant and Blueberry Tarts with Meringue

Makes eight 4-inch tarts

Preparation time: 35 minutes
Cooking time: 25 minutes

Pastry dough
2⅓ cups all-purpose flour, plus extra for dusting
1 teaspoon baking powder
1¾ sticks butter, plus extra for greasing
½ cup granulated sugar
2 teaspoons vanilla sugar (see page 10) or a few drops vanilla extract
1 egg

Filling
⅓ cup blueberry jelly
2 cups blueberries
2 cups red currants or other berries of your choice

Meringue
3 egg whites
¾ superfine sugar or granulated sugar
juice of ½ lemon

1 To make the pastry dough, mix together the flour and baking powder. Put the butter, granulated sugar, vanilla sugar or vanilla extract, and egg into a bowl and beat with an electric mixer until fluffy. Add the flour mixture and beat until a smooth dough forms.

2 Preheat the oven to 350°F. Grease eight 4-inch tart pans and dust with a little flour.

3 Roll out the dough on a work surface lightly dusted with flour to a thickness of about ¼ inch. Put the prepared pans close together and lay the dough over the tops. Press into the pans and use a knife to trim the edges level with the top of the pans. Bake in the preheated oven for about 15 minutes, then remove from the oven and let cool. Do not turn off the oven.

4 To make the filling, stir the jelly until smooth and brush over the pastry shells. Gently mix together the blueberries and red currants and divide among the pastry shells.

5 To make the meringue, beat the egg whites until they hold soft peaks, then add the sugar, little by little. Beat for an additional 5 minutes on the highest speed setting until the egg whites are glossy and hold stiff peaks. Add the lemon juice and stir to combine. Transfer the meringue mixture to a pastry bag fitted with a small tip and pipe dots of meringue onto the tarts.

6 Bake in the oven for 10 minutes, until the tips of the meringue are light brown. Remove from the oven and let cool before serving.

Gooseberry Meringue Cake

Makes one 10-inch cake

Preparation time: 40 minutes, plus 1 hour to rise
Cooking time: 1 hour 5 minutes

Cake
2 cups all-purpose flour, plus extra for dusting
¼ cup granulated sugar
pinch of salt
grated rind of lemon
2¼ teaspoons active dry yeast
½ cup lukewarm milk
1 egg, beaten
butter for greasing

Filling
2 cups low-fat fromage blanc, mascarpone, or ricotta cheese
2½ tablespoons cornstarch
⅔ cup granulated sugar
1 teaspoon vanilla sugar (see page 10) or a few drops vanilla extract
grated rind of 1 lemon
1 tablespoon lemon juice
2 eggs
pinch of salt
1 (16-ounce) can gooseberries or 3½ cups fresh gooseberries

Meringue
3 egg whites
⅔ cup superfine sugar or granulated sugar

1 To make the cake, sift the flour, sugar, salt, and lemon rind into a large bowl, then stir in the yeast. Make a well in the center.

2 Pour the milk and egg into the well in the dry ingredients and knead to a soft dough. Cover with a damp dish towel and let rise in a warm place for about 30 minutes, or until lightly risen and springy to the touch.

3 Meanwhile, to make the filling, put the fromage blanc, mascarpone, or ricotta cheese, cornstarch, granulated sugar, vanilla sugar or vanilla extract, lemon rind, lemon juice, eggs, and salt into a bowl and beat until smooth.

4 Preheat the oven to 350°F. Grease a 10-inch round, loose-bottom fluted tart pan and put onto a baking sheet.

5 Roll out the dough on a work surface lightly dusted with flour and use to line the bottom and sides of the prepared pan, pressing with your knuckles to fit the sides. Spread the cheese mixture over the bottom and level the surface, then sprinkle the gooseberries over the top, lightly pressing the fruit into the filling. Bake in the preheated oven for about 50 minutes.

6 Meanwhile, to make the meringue, beat the egg whites in an electric mixer until they hold soft peaks, then add the sugar, a little at a time. Beat for an additional 5 minutes on the highest speed setting until the egg white is glossy and hold stiff peaks.

7 Remove the cake from the oven and spread the meringue on top, then return to the oven and bake for an additional 15 minutes, until pale golden brown. Let the cake cool in the pan, then transfer to a plate to serve.

Plum and Puff Pastry Tart

Makes one 12 × 16 inch tart

Preparation time: 30 minutes, plus 15 minutes to chill
Cooking time: 35 minutes

Pastry dougb
butter, for greasing
2 sheets ready-to-bake puff pastry
all-purpose flour, for dusting

Filling
5–6 plums (about 12 ounces)
1 cup crème fraîche or mascarpone
⅓ cup granulated sugar
1 teaspoon vanilla sugar (see page 10) or a few drops vanilla extract
pinch of ground cinnamon
3 eggs
1 tablespoon cornstarch
2 tablespoons dried bread crumbs
4 ounces semisweet chocolate

1 Preheat the oven to 375°F. Grease a 12 x 16-inch baking pan.

2 Lay the pastry on a work surface, dust with flour, and roll out the pastry to a rectangle slightly larger than the pan. Lay the pastry on the pan, turn up the edge, and prick the bottom with a fork in several places. Chill in the refrigerator for about 15 minutes.

3 Meanwhile, to make the filling, halve and pit the plums. Put the crème fraîche or mascarpone, granulated sugar, vanilla sugar or vanilla extract, cinnamon, eggs, and cornstarch into a bowl and mix until smooth.

4 Sprinkle the bread crumbs over the pastry and cover with the filling mixture. Arrange the plums on top, lightly pressing them into the filling.

5 Bake the tart in the preheated oven for about 35 minutes, until golden brown. Remove from the oven and let cool in the pan.

6 Put the chocolate into a double boiler or a heatproof bowl set over a saucepan of gently simmering water and heat until melted. Drizzle the chocolate over the tart with a fork. Cut the tart into pieces, arrange on a plate, and serve.

Tip: This tart also tastes great made with apples, apricots, or peaches in season.

Yellow Plum and Puff Pastry Tart

Makes one 9½-inch tart

Preparation time: 30 minutes, plus 15 minutes to chill
Cooking time: 35 minutes

Pastry dough
butter, for greasing
1 sheet ready-to-bake puff pastry
all-purpose flour, for dusting

Filling
20 small yellow plums (about 14 ounces)
1 cup crème fraîche or mascarpone
½ cup granulated sugar
1 teaspoon vanilla sugar (see page 10) or a few drops vanilla extract
3 eggs
1 tablespoon cornstarch
1 tablespoon dried bread crumbs
confectioners' sugar, for dusting

1 Preheat the oven to 375°F. Grease a 9½-inch round tart pan.

2 Lay the pastry on a work surface, dust with flour, and roll out to a circle slightly larger than the prepared pan. Lay the pastry in the pan, turn up the edge, and prick the bottom with a fork in several places. Chill in the refrigerator for about 15 minutes.

3 Meanwhile, to make the filling, pit the plums. Put the crème fraîche or mascarpone, granulated sugar, vanilla sugar or vanilla extract, eggs, and cornstarch into a bowl and mix until smooth.

4 Sprinkle the bread crumbs over the pastry and cover with the filling mixture. Arrange the plums on top, lightly pressing them into the filling.

5 Bake in the preheated oven for about 35 minutes, until golden brown. Remove from the oven and let cool in the pan. Carefully remove the tart from the pan and transfer to a plate. Dust with confectioners' sugar just before serving.

Tip: This cake also tastes great made with apples, apricots, or peaches in season.

Plum Strudel

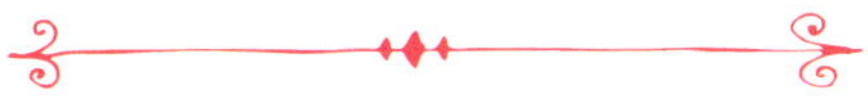

Makes one strudel

Preparation time: 30 minutes, plus 30 minutes to rest
Cooking time: 45 minutes

Pastry dough
½ cup cold water
pinch of salt
1 tablespoon sunflower oil, plus extra for brushing
1 egg yolk
2 cups all-purpose flour, plus extra for dusting
melted butter, for greasing
fruit brandy, such as plum brandy or apple brandy, for drizzling

Filling
6 plums (about 14 ounces)
1½ sticks butter
1 cup dried bread crumbs
¾ cup ground almonds
¾ cup granulated sugar
a pinch of ground cinnamon

1 To make the pastry dough, mix together the water, salt, oil, and egg yolk in a mixing bowl. Add the flour and mix until smooth. Cover the dough and let rest for 30 minutes.

2 Turn out the dough onto a dish towel lightly dusted with flour. Roll the dough out as thinly as possible, then, using your hands, gently stretch it out. Brush with oil and a little melted butter, then drizzle with the brandy.

3 Preheat the oven to 350°F. Grease a 12 x 16-inch baking pan.

4 To make the filling, pit the plums, cut them into small slices, and arrange on top of the pastry. Melt half the butter in a skillet, add the bread crumbs, and sauté until brown. Mix with the almonds, granulated sugar, and cinnamon and sprinkle the mixture over the plums.

5 Use the dish towel to roll up the pastry and lay it in the prepared baking pan. Bake in the preheated oven for about 45 minutes. Meanwhile, melt the remaining butter and use to brush the strudel shortly before the end of cooking. Dust with confectioners' sugar just before serving.

French Plum Cake

Makes one 8-inch cake

Preparation time: 25 minutes
Cooking time: 45 minutes

butter, for greasing
12 small plums (about 9 ounces)
3 eggs
⅓ cup granulated sugar
pinch of salt
¾ cup all-purpose flour
1¼ cups ground almonds (almond meal)
½ cup heavy cream
confectioners' sugar, for dusting

1 Preheat the oven to 350°F. Grease a deep 8-inch fluted tart pan.

2 Carefully halve and pit the plums, keeping the stems in place, if possible.

3 Put the eggs, sugar, and salt into a bowl and beat with an electric mixer until fluffy. Add the flour, 1 tablespoon at a time, and beat to combine. Add the almonds, then gradually add the cream, continuing to beat until a thick, smooth dough forms.

4 Transfer the dough to the prepared pan. Arrange the two halves of each plum together on top, stem ends pointing upward.

5 Bake in the preheated oven for about 45 minutes. Let cool, then remove from the pan. Dust with confectioners' sugar just before serving.

Tip: Apricots or blackberries can be used instead of plums. Because it has a slightly sharp flavor, this cake tastes good served with crème fraîche or Greek yogurt mixed with a little vanilla sugar (see page 10).

Apricot and Rice Tart

Makes one 11-inch tart

Preparation time: 45 minutes, plus 30 minutes to chill
Cooking time: 50–60 minutes

Pastry dough
1⅔ cups all-purpose flour, plus extra for dusting
pinch of salt
1 stick butter
1 egg
⅓ cup granulated sugar

Filling
1 vanilla bean
3 cups milk
1¼ cups short-grain rice
1 cup granulated sugar
grated rind and juice of 1 lemon
1 cinnamon stick
1 pound apricots
2 eggs, separated
pinch of salt
1 cup crème fraîche or mascarpone
confectioners' sugar, for dusting

1 To make the pastry dough, mix together the flour and salt on a work surface and make a well in the center. Cut the butter into small pieces and place in the well along with the egg and sugar. Knead until a smooth dough forms. Wrap in plastic wrap and chill in the refrigerator for 30 minutes.

2 To make the filling, halve the vanilla bean lengthwise and scrape out the seeds. Put the milk, rice, ¾ cup of the granulated sugar, lemon rind and juice, cinnamon stick, and vanilla bean and seeds into a saucepan and bring to a boil. Reduce the heat and simmer for about 20 minutes, stirring occasionally. Pour the mixture into a bowl, cover with plastic wrap, and let cool until lukewarm.

3 Preheat the oven to 350°F. Line an 11-inch tart pan with parchment paper. Put the dough on a work surface lightly dusted with flour, divide into two pieces, and press one piece over the bottom of the prepared pan. Roll the remaining piece into a log shape and press around the inner edge of the pan. Prick the bottom with a fork in several places.

4 Halve and pit the apricots. Beat the egg whites with the salt until they hold stiff peaks, gradually adding 2 tablespoons of the remaining granulated sugar. Mix together the egg yolks, crème fraîche, and remaining granulated sugar. Remove the cinnamon stick and vanilla bean from the rice. Mix the rice mixture with the egg mixture. Fold in the beaten egg whites.

5 Spread half the rice mixture in the pastry shell, then arrange half the apricots on top. Spread the remaining rice on top, followed by the remaining apricots.

6 Bake in the preheated oven for 50–60 minutes. If it is browning too quickly, cover with aluminum foil. Dust with confectioners' sugar before serving.

Apricot and Blueberry Cake

Makes one 12 × 16-inch cake

Preparation time: 45 minutes
Cooking time: 40 minutes

Crust
3⅔ cups all-purpose flour
1 cup granulated sugar
¼ cup vanilla sugar (see page 10) or a few drops vanilla extract
1¾ sticks butter, plus extra for greasing

Topping
1¼ sticks butter
⅔ cup granulated sugar
2 teaspoons vanilla sugar or a few drops vanilla extract
2 eggs
2 cups fromage blanc, mascarpone, or ricotta cheese
grated rind of 1 lemon
2 tablespoons lemon juice
1 envelope vanilla pudding and pie filling mix
1¾ pounds apricots
2 cups blueberries
confectioners' sugar, for dusting
heavy cream, to serve (optional)

1 Preheat the oven to 400°F. Grease a 12 x 16-inch baking pan.

2 To make the crust, mix together the flour, granulated sugar, vanilla sugar or vanilla extract, and butter in a mixing bowl. Cut the butter into small pieces and rub it in with your fingertips until a crumbly consistency is achieved. Spread two-thirds of the crumb mixture over the bottom of the prepared pan, pressing down firmly. Bake in the preheated oven for about 10 minutes. Remove from the oven and reduce the oven temperature to 350°F.

3 Meanwhile, to make the topping, put the butter, granulated sugar, and vanilla sugar or vanilla extract into a bowl and beat with an electric mixer until fluffy. Add the eggs, one at a time, beating after each addition until creamy. Stir the fromage blanc, mascarpone, or ricotta cheese, lemon rind and juice, and pudding and pie filling mix into the mixture. Spread over the crust.

4 Halve and pit the apricots. Arrange on top of the cream layer, alternating with the blueberries in diagonal stripes. Sprinkle the remaining crumb mixture on top of the fruit.

5 Bake the cake for 30 minutes. Let cool, then cut it into pieces, dust with confectioners' sugar, and serve with cream, if using.

Peach Upside-Down Tart

Makes one 9½-inch tart

Preparation time: 20 minutes
Cooking time: 15 minutes

6 peaches (about 2¼ pounds)
6 tablespoons butter
⅔ cup granulated sugar
2 teaspoons vanilla sugar (see page 10) or a few drops vanilla extract
2 sheets ready-to-bake puff pastry
heavy cream, to serve

1 Preheat the oven to 425°F.

2 Halve and pit the peaches. Melt the butter in a saucepan. Sprinkle the bottom of a 9½-inch ovenproof skillet with the granulated sugar. Arrange the peach halves on top in a tightly packed circle, cut edges facing downward. Drizzle the melted butter evenly over the peaches, then sprinkle the vanilla sugar or vanilla extract on top.

3 Put the skillet over medium heat to caramelize the sugar, tilting the pan slightly to keep the peach halves moving.

4 Roll out the pastry into a 1-inch-thick circle slightly larger than the skillet. Cover the peaches with the pastry, pressing down the edges and trimming any excess.

5 Bake in the middle of the preheated oven for about 15 minutes, until golden brown. If the pastry starts to brown too quickly, cover it with aluminum foil.

6 Remove from the oven and turn out onto a plate. Serve warm with heavy cream.

Sour Cream Cake with Nectarines

Makes one 10-inch cake

Preparation time: 30 minutes
Cooking time: 1 hour 5 minutes

butter, for greasing
½ cup dried bread crumbs
3 nectarines
3 cups low-fat fromage blanc, mascarpone, or ricotta cheese
½ cup sour cream
3 eggs
¾ cup granulated sugar
1 envelope vanilla pudding and pie filling mix
½ cup sunflower oil
½ cup milk
½ cup ground almonds (almond meal)
confectioners' sugar, for dusting

1 Preheat the oven to 325°F. Grease a 10-inch round springform pan and sprinkle with the bread crumbs.

2 Pit the nectarines, then cut them into thin slices.

3 Put the fromage blanc, mascarpone, or ricotta cheese into a mixing bowl with the sour cream, eggs, sugar, vanilla pudding and pie filling mix, oil, milk, and almonds, then beat with an electric mixer until smooth and creamy.

4 Spoon the batter into the prepared pan and arrange the nectarine slices in a circle on top. Bake in the preheated oven for about 1 hour 5 minutes.

5 Remove from the oven and let cool in the pan, then carefully turn out of the pan and transfer to a plate. Dust with confectioners' sugar just before serving.

Cherry Marble Cake

Makes one 10-inch cake

Preparation time: 30 minutes
Cooking time: 1 hour

2 tablespoons dried bread crumbs
2¼ sticks butter, softened, plus extra for greasing
1¼ cups granulated sugar
2 teaspoons vanilla sugar *(see page 10)* *or a few drops vanilla extract*
4 eggs
4 cups all-purpose flour
2 teaspoons baking powder
½ teaspoon salt
½ cup milk
2 cups pitted sweet fresh cherries
⅓ cup unsweetened cocoa powder
confectioners' sugar, for dusting

1 Preheat the oven to 350°F. Grease a deep 10-inch fluted tube pan and sprinkle with the bread crumbs.

2 Put the butter into a bowl and beat until creamy, gradually adding the granulated sugar and vanilla sugar or vanilla extract. Add the eggs, one at a time, beating after each addition, until smooth.

3 Mix the flour with the baking powder and salt. Gradually add to the butter mixture, alternating with the milk, beating until the batter is thick and smooth.

4 Spoon half the batter into the prepared pan. Spread half of the cherries over the cake batter, pressing them in slightly. Stir the cocoa powder into the remaining batter.

5 Spoon the cocoa batter over the cherries, then sprinkle the remaining cherries on top. Using the handle of a wooden spoon, gently swirl the two layers together to produce a marbled effect.

6 Bake in the preheated oven for about 1 hour. Let cool in the pan for 5 minutes, then turn out onto a wire rack to cool completely. Transfer to a plate and dust with confectioners' sugar just before serving.

Cherry Clafoutis

Makes one 11-inch clafoutis

Preparation time: 45 minutes, plus 30 minutes to rest
Cooking time: 20 minutes

2 eggs, separated
⅓ cup granulated sugar
1 tablespoon vanilla sugar (see page 10) or a few drops vanilla extract
¾ cup all-purpose flour
¾ cup milk
pinch of salt
pinch of grated lemon rind
2 tablespoons vegetable oil
1⅔ cups pitted sweet fresh cherries
confectioners' sugar, for dusting
whipped cream, to serve (optional)

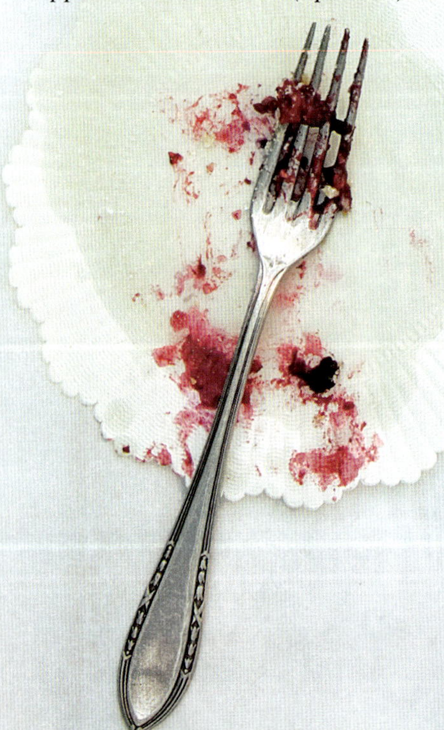

1 Put the egg yolks, granulated sugar, and vanilla sugar or vanilla extract into a large bowl and beat with an electric mixer until fluffy. Add the flour, milk, salt, and lemon rind and beat until smooth. Let rest for 30 minutes.

2 Preheat the oven to 350°F.

3 Beat the egg whites until they hold stiff peaks, then carefully fold them into the batter.

4 Heat the oil in an 11-inch ovenproof skillet. Pour in the batter and cook over low heat for 5 minutes, until the underside is lightly browned. Sprinkle the cherries over the surface.

5 Transfer the skillet to the preheated oven and bake for about 15 minutes. Slide the clafoutis out of the pan onto a cake plate. Dust with confectioners' sugar and serve lukewarm with whipped cream, if using.

Grandma's Cherry Cake

Makes one 12 × 16-inch cake

Preparation time: 25 minutes
Cooking time: 1 hour

2 tablespoons dried bread crumbs
1¼ sticks butter, softened, plus extra for greasing
¾ cup granulated sugar
4 eggs, separated
¾ cup ground almonds (almond meal)
1¼ cups all-purpose flour
½ teaspoon baking powder
3 cups pitted fresh sweet cherries
confectioners' sugar, for dusting

1 Preheat the oven to 350°F. Grease a 12 x 16-inch rectangular cake pan and sprinkle with the bread crumbs.

2 Put the butter and sugar into a large bowl and beat with an electric mixer until fluffy. Add the egg yolks, one at a time, beating after each addition until combined. Beat the egg whites until they hold stiff peaks. Stir the almonds, flour, and baking powder into the butter mixture, then fold in the beaten egg whites.

3 Spoon the batter into the prepared pan and spread the cherries on top.

4 Bake on the bottom shelf of the preheated oven for 50 minutes. At the end of the cooking time, turn off the oven and let the cake rest inside for 10 minutes.

5 Remove from the oven and let cool in the pan. Turn out of the pan, dust with confectioners' sugar, and serve.

Apple and Cider Tart

Makes one 10-inch tart

Preparation time: 45 minutes
Cooking time: 35 minutes

Pastry dough
2⅓ cups all-purpose flour, plus extra for dusting
1 teaspoon baking powder
1 stick butter, plus extra for greasing
⅔ cup low-fat fromage blanc, mascarpone, or ricotta cheese
½ cup milk
⅓ cup granulated sugar
1 teaspoon vanilla sugar (see page 10) or a few drops vanilla extract
pinch of salt

Filling
1 envelope vanilla pudding and pie filling mix
2 eggs, separated
1½ cups milk
½ cup granulated sugar
⅔ cup hard apple cider or apple juice
pinch of salt
7 Golden Delicious apples (about 1¾ pounds)
juice of ½ lemon
whipped cream, to serve (optional)

1 Preheat the oven to 350°F. Grease a 10-inch round tart pan.

2 To make the pastry dough, mix together the flour and the baking powder. Melt the butter in a saucepan. Put the flour mixture into the bowl of a food mixer with the fromage blanc, mascarpone, or ricotta cheese, milk, butter, granulated sugar, vanilla sugar or vanilla extract, and salt and mix to a smooth dough. Roll out the dough on a work surface lightly dusted with flour to a circle slightly larger than the pan. Line the prepared pan with the dough, turning up the edge.

3 To make the filling, mix the pudding and pie filling mix with the egg yolks and ¼ cup of the milk. Pour the remaining milk into a saucepan with ⅓ cup of the sugar and bring to a boil. Pour in the pudding mixture, stirring, and bring back to a boil. Add the cider or apple juice and bring back to a boil. Transfer the mixture to a bowl, cover with plastic wrap, and let cool in the refrigerator until lukewarm.

4 Meanwhile, beat the egg whites with the salt until they hold stiff peaks, then fold into the lukewarm vanilla pudding mixture. Spread the mixture over the dough and level the surface.

5 Peel, core, and quarter the apples and cut them into thin slices. Mix the apple slices with the remaining sugar and the lemon juice, then arrange on top of the vanilla pudding mixture in a circular pattern.

6 Bake in the preheated oven for about 35 minutes, until golden brown. Let cool before serving with whipped cream, if using.

Individual Apple Pies

Makes four 4-inch pies

Preparation time: 1 hour, plus 30 minutes to chill
Cooking time: 45–50 minutes

1½ sticks cold butter, plus extra for greasing
2⅓ cups all-purpose flour, plus extra for dusting
pinch of salt
7 Granny Smith or other cooking apples (about 2¼ pounds)
¾ cup granulated sugar
pinch of nutmeg
½ teaspoon ground cinnamon
grated rind of 1 lemon
1 egg yolk
3½ tablespoons heavy cream
vanilla ice cream, to serve

1 To make the pastry dough, cut 1 stick of the butter into small pieces. Put 2½ cups of the flour, the salt, and the pieces of butter into a food processor and process until a crumbly dough forms. Gradually add a few tablespoonfuls of cold water and continue to process until the dough forms a ball. Wrap the dough in plastic wrap and chill in the refrigerator for about 30 minutes.

2 Preheat the oven to 400°F. Grease four 4-inch tart pans.

3 To make the filling, peel and core the apples and cut into slices. Mix the apple slices with the sugar, nutmeg, cinnamon, lemon rind, and the remaining flour.

4 Roll out two-thirds of the dough on a work surface lightly dusted with flour to a thickness of ⅛ inch and use to line the prepared pans. Prick the bottoms with a fork in several places. Divide the apple mixture among the pans and dot with the remaining butter.

5 Roll out one-third of the remaining dough and cut into strips. Thinly roll out the remaining dough to make four pastry lids and place these on top of the filling, sealing well around the edges. Pierce a few holes in the pastry lids. Beat together the egg yolk and the cream. Lay the pastry strips on top of the lids in a crisscross pattern and brush with the egg yolk-and-cream mixture.

6 Bake in the preheated oven for about 45–50 minutes. Serve lukewarm with vanilla ice cream, or cold.

Cinnamon, Apple, and Almond Cake

Makes one 9½-inch cake

Preparation time: 45 minutes
Cooking time: 45 minutes

Cake
3¼ cups all-purpose flour, plus extra for dusting
2 teaspoons baking powder
2¼ sticks butter, plus extra for greasing
⅔ cup granulated sugar
4 eggs
pinch of salt
½ cup milk

Topping
9 Pippin or other sweet crisp apples (about 2¼ pounds)
juice of ½ lemon
½ teaspoon ground cinnamon
¼ cup granulated sugar
¾ cup slivered almonds
confectioners' sugar, for dusting

1 Preheat the oven to 350°F. Grease a 9½-inch round springform pan and dust with flour.

2 To make the cake, mix together the flour and the baking powder. Put the butter into a large bowl and beat with an electric mixer until fluffy, gradually beating in the sugar, eggs, salt, and flour mixture. Add the milk, a little at a time, beating after each addition until smooth.

3 Spoon the batter into the prepared pan and level the surface with a spatula.

4 To make the topping, peel, quarter, and core the apples. Cut the quarters into thin slices and drizzle with the lemon juice. Dust the apple slices with the cinnamon and mix with the sugar and almonds.

5 Spread the apple mixture evenly on top of the cake batter. Bake in the preheated oven for about 45 minutes. Remove from the oven and let cool. Unclip and release the springform, transfer the cake to a plate, dust with confectioners' sugar, and serve.

Apple and Cinnamon Cake

Makes one 11-inch cake

Preparation time: 45 minutes
Cooking time: 30 minutes

Cake
1¼ cups all-purpose flour
⅔ cup cornstarch
2 teaspoons baking powder
1¼ sticks butter, softened, plus extra for greasing
⅔ cup granulated sugar
1 teaspoon confectioners' sugar
4 eggs

Topping
7 Pippin or other sweet crisp apples (about 1¾ pounds)
3 tablespoons granulated sugar
1 teaspoon ground cinnamon

1 Preheat the oven to 350°F. Grease an 11-inch tart pan or pie plate.

2 To make the cake, mix together the flour, cornstarch, and baking powder. Put the butter into a large bowl and beat with an electric mixer until fluffy. Gradually add the granulated sugar and confectioners' sugar, then add the eggs, one at a time, beating after each addition until combined. Add the flour mixture in two batches and mix to combine.

3 Spoon the batter into the prepared pan and level the surface.

4 To make the topping, peel and core the apples and cut them into thin slices. Mix the apple slices with the sugar and cinnamon. Spread the apple slices evenly over the batter.

5 Bake in the preheated oven for about 30 minutes, until lightly browned. Let cool in the pan, then cut into wedges and serve.

Grape and Sour Cream Flan

Makes one 10-inch flan

Preparation time: 40 minutes
Cooking time: 50 minutes

Pastry dough
butter, for greasing
2¼ cups all-purpose flour, plus extra for dusting
1 teaspoon baking powder
⅔ cup low-fat fromage blanc, mascarpone, or ricotta cheese
3½ tablespoons milk
3½ tablespoons vegetable oil
⅓ cup granulated sugar
1 teaspoon vanilla sugar (see page 10) or a few drops vanilla extract
pinch of salt

Filling
1 cup sour cream
2 egg yolks
1¾ cups milk
1 envelope vanilla pudding and pie filling mix
1 teaspoon vanilla sugar or a few drops vanilla extract
¼ cup granulated sugar
2 cups mixed red and white grapes

1 Preheat the oven to 350°F. Grease a 10-inch tart pan and line with parchment paper.

2 To make the pastry dough, mix together the flour and the baking powder. Put the mixture into the bowl of a food mixer with the fromage blanc, mascarpone, or ricotta cheese, milk, oil, granulated sugar, vanilla sugar or vanilla extract, and salt and work to a smooth dough using the dough hook.

3 Turn out the dough onto a work surface lightly dusted with flour and roll out to a 10-inch circle, then place it in the prepared pan, turning it up at the edge.

4 To make the filling, mix the sour cream with the egg yolks. Mix ½ cup of the milk with the pudding and pie filling mix. Pour the remaining milk into a saucepan and add the vanilla sugar or vanilla extract and granulated sugar, then bring to a boil. Stir the pudding mixture into the pan and bring to a boil. Remove from the heat and stir the pudding mixture into the sour cream mixture. Let cool slightly.

5 Spread the cream filling over the pastry shell. Arrange the grapes on top of the cream filling.

6 Bake in the preheated oven for about 50 minutes, covering it with aluminum foil after 30 minutes. Let cool completely before serving.

Tip: To make a glaze, bring 1 cup white grape juice to a boil in a saucepan with 3 tablespoons granulated sugar. Add three sheets of soaked and squeezed gelatin and let dissolve. Let cool until it starts to set. Pour over the cake and let stand until the glaze is fully set.

Banana and Chocolate Flan

Makes one 11-inch flan

Preparation time: 55 minutes, plus 3 hours to chill

Crust

6 ounces semisweet chocolate
1½ tablespoons butter
10 cups chocolate puffed rice cereal

Topping

2½ cups low-fat fromage blanc, mascarpone, or ricotta cheese
½ cup granulated sugar
1 teaspoon vanilla sugar (see page 10) or a few drops vanilla extract
grated rind of 1 lemon
3 ripe bananas (¾ pound peeled weight)
2 tablespoons lemon juice
10 sheets gelatin
1 cup heavy cream
8 ounces semisweet chocolate shavings

1 To make the crust, break the chocolate into pieces, put it into a double boiler or a heatproof bowl set over a saucepan of gently simmering water, add the butter, and heat until melted, stirring continuously. Process the cereal in a food processor and stir into the chocolate mixture.

2 Line an 11-inch round springform pan with parchment paper. Spoon the chocolate mixture into the prepared pan, pressing down well with the back of the spoon. Let chill in the refrigerator for 1 hour.

3 To make the topping, mix together the fromage blanc, mascarpone, or ricotta cheese, granulated sugar, vanilla sugar or vanilla extract, and lemon rind in a bowl. Thinly slice the bananas and drizzle with the lemon juice. Soak the gelatin in cold water for 10 minutes, then gently squeeze out the water. Put the gelatin into a saucepan with a little water and stir over medium heat until dissolved. Add the bananas and gelatin to the cheese mixture.

4 Whip the cream until it holds soft peaks, then use a spatula to fold it into the setting cheese and banana mixture. Spread the mixture over the crust and level the surface with a spatula. Let chill in the refrigerator for 2 hours.

5 Sprinkle the chocolate shavings over the flan. Unclip and release the springform, transfer the flan to a plate, and serve.

Pineapple and Coconut Cake

Makes one 11-inch cake

Preparation time: 50 minutes
Cooking time: 1 hour 20 minutes

Cake
6 cups freshly grated coconut
1¾ cups coconut milk
4 eggs, separated
1½ cups firmly packed light brown sugar
1⅔ cups all-purpose flour
⅔ cup cornstarch
2 teaspoons baking powder
½ teaspoon ground cardamom
½ teaspoon ground cinnamon
1¼ cups ground almonds

Topping
½ pineapple
½ cup ginger preserves
½ cup freshly grated coconut

1 Preheat the oven to 325°F. Line an 11-inch round springform pan with parchment paper.

2 To make the topping, peel and quarter the pineapple and cut out the hard center. Cut the quarters into ⅛ inch-thick slices and set aside until required.

3 To make the cake, put the coconut into a blender with the coconut milk, in batches, and process until the coconut is finely ground. Transfer the coconut mixture to a bowl.

4 Put the egg yolks into a bowl with half the sugar and beat with an electric mixer until fluffy. Add the coconut mixture and mix to combine. Mix together the flour, cornstarch, baking powder, cardamom, cinnamon, and almonds. Stir the flour mixture into the coconut mixture. Put the egg whites into a separate bowl and beat until they hold stiff peaks, adding the remaining sugar a little at a time. Carefully fold into the coconut mixture.

5 Spoon the batter into the prepared pan and arrange the pineapple slices on top in a fan arrangement. Bake in the preheated oven for about 80 minutes, until golden brown. Let cool slightly, then remove from the pan and transfer to a wire rack to cool completely.

6 Heat the preserves in a saucepan over low heat, then pass it through a strainer and use to brush the top of the cake. Sprinkle the grated coconut over the top just before serving.

Tip: Fresh coconut slices are often available in the fresh fruit section of supermarkets. Alternatively, pour 1 cup hot water over 4 cups dried coconut and let soak for 10 minutes.

Pomegranate Cheesecake

Makes one 9½-inch cheesecake

Preparation time: 30 minutes, plus 4½ hours to chill

Crust
8 ounces oatmeal cookies or other plain cookies
6 tablespoons butter, plus extra for greasing

Filling
9 sheets gelatin
2 cups cream cheese
3 tablespoons orange juice
⅔ cup confectioners' sugar
1 cup heavy cream
2 egg whites

Topping
2 sheets gelatin
3½ cup pomegranate juice
3 tablespoons kirsch or other cherry liqueur
¼ cup granulated sugar
2 pomegranates, seeds scraped out

1 Grease a 9½-inch round springform pan. Put the cookies into a plastic bag and crush with a rolling pin until reduced to fine crumbs. Melt the butter in a saucepan, add the cookie crumbs, and mix well. Press the mixture into the bottom of the prepared pan, then chill in the refrigerator for 30 minutes.

2 To make the filling, soak the gelatin in cold water for 10 minutes. Mix together the cream cheese, orange juice, and confectioners' sugar in a large bowl and gradually stir in the cream. Put the egg whites into a separate bowl and beat until they hold stiff peaks. Gently squeeze the water out of the gelatin. Put the gelatin into a saucepan over medium heat and stir until dissolved. Stir the gelatin into the cream cheese mixture and carefully fold in the egg whites.

3 Pour the filling into the pan, level the surface, cover with plastic wrap, and chill in the refrigerator for 2 hours.

4 Meanwhile, to make the topping, soak the gelatin in cold water for 10 minutes. Put the pomegranate juice into a saucepan with the kirsch and sugar and bring to a boil. Gently squeeze the water out of the gelatin and dissolve the gelatin in the pomegranate juice mixture. Remove from the heat, add the pomegranate seeds and let cool.

5 Spread the pomegranate gelatin over the set cheesecake and chill for 2 hours. Remove the cake from the pan and transfer to a plate to serve.

Yeast Cake with Mango

Makes one 12 × 16-inch cake

Preparation time: 35 minutes, plus approx. 30 minutes to rise
Cooking time: 40-45 minutes

Cake
3⅔ cups all-purpose flour, plus extra for dusting
⅓ cup granulated sugar
pinch of salt
2¼ teaspoons active dry yeast
1 cup lukewarm milk
grated rind of ½ lemon
2 eggs, beaten
5 tablespoons butter, softened, plus extra for greasing

Topping
2 ripe mangoes
2 tablespoons butter, softened
1 egg, separated
¼ cup firmly packed brown sugar
⅔ cup low-fat fromage blanc, mascarpone, or ricotta cheese
2 tablespoons all-purpose flour
grated rind of ½ lemon
pinch of salt
2 egg yolks, beaten
¼ cup dried coconut

1 To make the cake, sift the flour, sugar, and salt into a large bowl then stir in the yeast. Make a well in the center.

2 Add the milk, lemon rind, eggs, and butter to the dry ingredients and knead to a soft dough. Cover with a damp dish towel and let rise in a warm place for about 30 minutes, until risen and springy to the touch.

3 Preheat the oven to 350°F. Grease a 12 x 16-inch baking pan.

4 To make the topping, peel the mangoes, cut the flesh away from the pits, and cut into thin slices. Put the butter into a bowl and beat with an electric mixer until fluffy. Add the egg yolk and sugar, a little at a time, beating after each addition until combined. Mix in the fromage blanc, mascarpone, or ricotta cheese, flour, and lemon rind. Beat the egg white with the salt in a separate bowl until it holds stiff peaks, then fold into the cheese mixture.

5 Turn out the dough onto a work surface dusted with flour and roll out to a 12 x 16-inch rectangle. Lay it in the prepared pan, spread the cheese mixture evenly over the dough, and arrange the mango slices on top.

6 Brush the cake with the beaten egg yolk and bake in the preheated oven for about 45 minutes, until golden brown. Let cool, then sprinkle with the coconut and serve.

Chilled Buttermilk and Kiwi Flan

Makes one 11-inch flan

Preparation time: 35 minutes, plus 3 hours to chill
Cooking time: 25 minutes

Choux pastry dough
1 cup water
4½ tablespoons butter
pinch of salt
2½ tablespoons granulated sugar
1¼ cups all-purpose flour
3 eggs

Filling
14 sheets gelatin
4 cups buttermilk
juice of 2 lemons
½ cup granulated sugar
2 teaspoons vanilla sugar (see page 10) or a few drops vanilla extract
1 cup heavy cream
4 large kiwi, sliced

1 Preheat the oven to 425°F. Line a large baking sheet with parchment paper.

2 To make the choux pastry dough, put the water, butter, salt, and sugar into a saucepan and bring to a boil. Add the flour and stir vigorously with a wooden spoon until the mixture comes away from the bottom of the pan in a lump, leaving a white film. Remove from the heat and add the eggs, one at a time, beating with an electric mixer after each addition until combined.

3 Put the dough into a pastry bag fitted with a medium tip and pipe onto the prepared baking sheet from a distance of ⅜ inch to make a spiral with a diameter of 11 inches. Pipe any remaining dough in strips next to the spiral. Place the baking sheet on the middle shelf of the preheated oven and pour a small heatproof cup of water onto the floor of the oven. Bake for 25 minutes, until golden brown. Remove from the oven and transfer to a wire rack to cool.

4 To make the filling, soak the gelatin in cold water for 10 minutes. Mix together the buttermilk, lemon juice, granulated sugar, and vanilla sugar or vanilla extract. Squeeze the water out of the gelatin, put the gelatin into a saucepan with a little water, and heat over low heat, stirring continuously, until dissolved. Stir into the buttermilk mixture. Chill the mixture until it starts to set. Whip the cream until it holds stiff peaks and fold into the buttermilk mixture in two batches.

5 Clip an 11-inch round springform ring around the choux pastry spiral. Pour in the filling and spread evenly. Chill for 3 hours.

6 Break the baked strips of pastry into pieces. Arrange the kiwi on top of the flan and sprinkle with the pastry pieces. Unclip and release the springform and transfer the flan to a serving plate.

Mandarin Cheesecake

Makes one 8½-inch cheesecake

Preparation time: 30 minutes, plus 3½ hours to chill and 1 hour to stand

Crust
12 ladyfingers
1 stick butter

Filling
1 (28-ounce) can mandarin segments
2⅔ cups cream cheese
1½ cups plain yogurt
3 tablespoons orange juice
⅔ cup Italian aperitif, such as Campari®
10 sheets gelatin
½ cup granulated sugar

1 Line the bottom of an 8½-inch round springform pan with parchment paper and close the springform around it.

2 To make the crust, put the ladyfingers into a plastic bag and crush with a rolling pin until reduced to fine crumbs. Reserve 2 tablespoons for the decoration. Melt the butter in a saucepan, pour it over the remaining crumbs, and mix until combined. Spoon the mixture into the prepared pan, spreading it over the bottom and pressing down firmly. Chill in the refrigerator for 30 minutes.

3 To make the filling, carefully drain the mandarin segments, reserving half the juice. Put the cream cheese into a food processor with the yogurt, orange juice, and aperitif and blend until smooth.

4 Soak the gelatin in cold water for about 10 minutes. Put the sugar and the reserved juice into a saucepan and bring to a boil. Squeeze the water out of the gelatin, then add the gelatin to the pan and heat, stirring continuously, until dissolved. Remove from the heat and let stand for about 1 hour.

5 Gradually mix the gelatin mixture into the cream cheese mixture. Carefully mix in half the mandarin segments and spoon the mixture into the pan. Level the surface, cover with plastic wrap, and chill in the refrigerator for 3 hours.

6 Remove the plastic wrap and unclip and release the springform. Arrange the remaining mandarin segments on top of the cake and sprinkle the reserved crumbs on top.

Tip: The cheesecake can be made with fresh strawberries in summer. It can also be made with canned peach slices if mandarin segments are not available.

Angela's Orange Tart

Makes one 9½-inch tart

Preparation time: 35 minutes, plus 1 hour to chill
Cooking time: 1 hour 5 minutes

Pastry dough
1¼ sticks butter, diced, plus extra for greasing
2 cups all-purpose flour, plus extra for dusting
3 tablespoons granulated sugar
pinch of salt
1 egg
grated rind of ½ orange
2 tablespoons lukewarm water

Filling
1 egg
3 egg yolks
⅔ cup granulated sugar
1¾ cups crème fraîche or ricotta cheese
grated rind and juice of 1 orange
3 tablespoons orange marmalade
strips of orange zest, for decorating

1 To make the pastry dough, put the butter, flour, sugar, salt, egg, orange rind, and water into a large bowl and knead until a soft dough forms. Wrap the pastry in plastic wrap and chill in the refrigerator for at least 1 hour.

2 Preheat the oven to 350°F. Grease a 9½-inch fluted tart pan.

3 To make the filling, put the egg, egg yolks, and sugar into a bowl and beat with an electric mixer until fluffy. Put the crème fraîche or ricotta cheese into a saucepan and heat over low heat, beating continuously with a wire whisk. Mix in the orange rind and juice.

4 Add the hot orange mixture to the egg mixture and mix well. Pass through a fine strainer into a bowl and let cool.

5 Roll out the pastry dough on a work surface dusted with flour to a thickness of ⅛ inch. Use to line the prepared pan, trimming any surplus with a knife. Prick the bottom with a fork in several places.

6 Line with parchment paper, fill with pie weights or dried beans, and bake on the bottom shelf of the preheated oven for 15 minutes. Remove the weights and paper and bake for another 15 minutes. Remove from the oven and reduce the oven temperature to 325°F.

7 Brush the bottom of the pastry shell with the marmalade. Pour the orange mixture into the hot pastry shell and bake for an additional 35 minutes. Remove from the oven and let cool. Sprinkle with the orange zest just before serving.

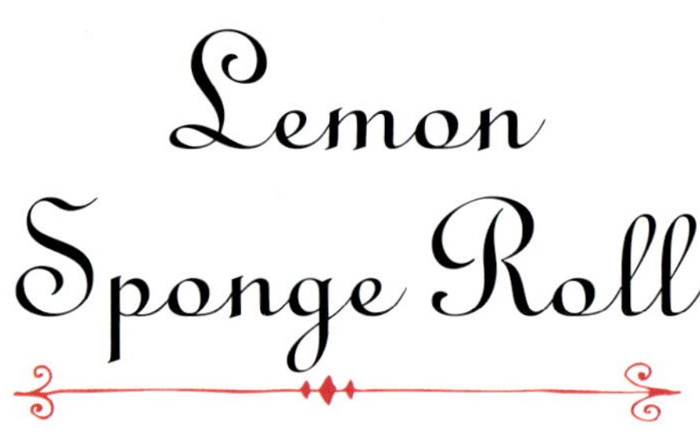

Lemon Sponge Roll

Makes one 16-inch roll

Preparation time: 50 minutes, plus 5 hours to cool and chill
Cooking time: 20 minutes

Sponge
5 eggs, separated
¼ cup lukewarm water
⅓ cup granulated sugar
¾ cup all-purpose flour
⅓ cup cornstarch
1 teaspoon baking powder

Filling
juice of 3 lemons
grated rind of 1 lemon
⅓ cup granulated sugar
1½ cups water
5 sheets gelatin
1 cup heavy cream
confectioners' sugar, for dusting
1 cup blueberries, to decorate

1 Preheat the oven to 325°F. Line a 12 × 16-inch baking pan with parchment paper.

2 To make the sponge, put the egg whites into a large bowl with the water and beat until they hold stiff peaks. Gradually add the sugar, stirring continuously, until combined. Beat the egg yolks and carefully fold in. Sift together the flour, cornstarch, and baking powder into the egg mixture and fold in carefully.

3 Spread the batter evenly in the prepared pan and bake on the middle shelf of the preheated oven for about 20 minutes.

4 Remove from the oven and immediately turn out onto a damp dish towel. Brush the parchment paper with cold water and peel off quickly. Use the dish towel to roll up the sponge from the long side, then let cool for 2 hours.

5 To make the filling, put the lemon juice, lemon rind, sugar, and water into a saucepan, bring to a boil, boil briefly, then remove from the heat. Soak the gelatin in a little cold water for 10 minutes, then squeeze out the water. Stir the gelatin into the warm lemon syrup and let cool.

6 Whip the cream until it holds stiff peaks. As soon as the lemon mixture begins to set, fold in the cream.

7 Carefully unroll the sponge and spread with the lemon cream. Roll up again immediately and chill in the refrigerator for 3 hours.

8 Just before serving, dust the roll with the confectioners' sugar, cut into slices, and decorate with the blueberries.

Angela's Lemon Tart

Makes one 9½-inch tart

Preparation time: 25 minutes, plus 30 minutes to chill
Cooking time: 1 hour 5 minutes

Pastry dough
1⅔ cups all-purpose flour, plus extra for dusting
¾ cup confectioners' sugar
1 cup ground almonds (almond meal)
1¼ sticks butter, plus extra for greasing
1 egg
pinch of salt

Filling
grated rind and juice of 3 lemons
1¼ sticks butter
1⅓ cups granulated sugar
4 eggs

Topping
2 lemons, thinly sliced
½ cup water
½ cup granulated sugar

1 To make the pastry dough, mix together the flour, confectioners' sugar and almonds. Melt the butter in a saucepan. Combine the flour mixture with the butter, egg, and salt in a food processer, then knead by hand until a smooth dough forms, wrap in plastic wrap, and chill in the refrigerator for 30 minutes.

2 Preheat the oven to 350°F. Grease a 9½-inch round tart pan.

3 To make the filling, put the lemon rind and juice, butter, and sugar into a saucepan over low heat and heat, stirring continuously, until the sugar has dissolved. Whisk the eggs with a wire whisk until frothy, then add them to the lemon mixture. Remove from the heat and continue stirring until smooth and creamy.

4 Roll out the dough on a work surface lightly dusted with flour into a ¼ inch-thick circle. Lay it in the tart pan, pressing it into place and trimming off any surplus with a sharp knife. Prick the bottom with a fork in several places.

5 Line with parchment paper, fill with pie weights or dried beans, and bake on the bottom shelf of the preheated oven for 15 minutes. Remove the weights and paper and bake for another 15 minutes. Remove from the oven and reduce the oven temperature to 275°F. Pour the filling into the pastry shell and bake for an additional 35 minutes. Transfer to a wire rack to cool.

6 Meanwhile, to make the topping, put the lemon slices into a shallow saucepan, add the water and sugar, bring to a boil, and simmer for 10 minutes. Remove from the heat and let cool.

7 Arrange the lemon slices on top of the tart and serve.

Fig and Orange Liqueur Cake

Makes one 9½-inch cake

Preparation time: 40 minutes
Cooking time: 40 minutes

Cake
8 dried figs
1 stick butter, plus extra for greasing
½ vanilla bean
4 eggs, separated
¾ cup granulated sugar
3 tablespoons cornstarch
2¼ cups ground almonds (almond meal)
4 teaspoons orange liqueur

Topping
8 fresh figs
1 cup heavy cream
⅓ cup confectioners' sugar, plus extra for dusting
3 tablespoons slivered almonds, toasted, for sprinkling

1 Preheat the oven to 400°F. Grease a 9½-inch round springform pan.

2 To make the cake, finely chop the dried figs. Melt the butter in a small saucepan. Halve the vanilla bean lengthwise and scrape out the seeds.

3 Put the egg yolks into a bowl with with ½ cup of the sugar and the vanilla seeds and beat with an electric mixer until fluffy. Add the cornstarch, dried figs, almonds, melted butter, and liqueur and mix to combine.

4 Beat the egg whites in a separate bowl until they hold soft peaks. Add the remaining sugar, a little at a time, beating until the egg white holds stiff peaks. Carefully fold into the fig mixture.

5 Spoon the batter into the prepared pan and bake on the middle shelf of the preheated oven for 40 minutes. Remove from the oven and let cool completely. Unclip and release the springform and transfer the cake to a plate.

6 To make the topping, halve the fresh figs. Put the cream into a bowl, add the confectioners' sugar, and whip until it holds stiff peaks. Spread the cream on top of the cake and arrange the figs on top of the cream. Sprinkle with the almonds and dust with confectioners' sugar.

Tip: Arrange some fig leaves on the plate and lay the cake on top of them to serve.

Sherry Trifle with Tipsy Fruit

Makes eight small trifles

Preparation time: 45 minutes, plus time to stand

1 envelope vanilla pudding and pie filling mix
2 cups milk
20 ladyfingers (about 9 ounces)
⅓ cup apricot preserves
1 cup dry sherry
2 oranges
2 nectarines
1 ripe banana
1 vanilla bean
1 cup heavy cream
3 tablespoons granulated sugar

1 Prepare the vanilla pudding and pie filling mix with the milk according to the package directions, pour into a bowl, cover with plastic wrap, and let cool for 1 hour.

2 Break up the ladyfingers into chunks and place in a shallow bowl. Mix the preserves with ⅔ cup of the sherry, carefully mix with the ladyfinger pieces, cover with plastic wrap, and set aside.

3 Cut off ⅜ -inch slice from the top and bottom of each orange. Peel the oranges, removing both the outer skin and the white pith. Cut with a small knife inside the skin of each orange segment and separate the flesh from the skins. Collect any orange juice in a bowl.

4 Halve and pit the nectarines and cut into small pieces. Cut the banana in half lengthwise, then cut into thin slices. Mix with the orange segments and nectarine pieces. Pour the remaining sherry over the top and let soak for 30 minutes.

5 Divide the ladyfinger mixture among eight glass dishes and spoon the fruit and orange juice over them, reserving some fruit to decorate.

6 Halve the vanilla bean lengthwise and scrape out the seeds. Whip the cream with the vanilla seeds and sugar until it holds stiff peaks. Whisk the pudding mixture with a wire whisk until smooth, then fold in the cream.

7 Spoon the cream mixture into the dishes and tap the dishes on the work surface to help the mixture to settle. Decorate with the remaining fruit pieces and serve chilled.

Tamarillo Cake with Chocolate

Makes one 9½-inch cake

Preparation time: 45 minutes,
plus 4 hours to cool
Cooking time: 50 minutes

Cake
butter, for greasing
5 eggs, separated
pinch of salt
3 tablespoons water
¾ cup granulated sugar
¾ cup all-purpose flour
3 tablespoons cornstarch
½ cup unsweetened cocoa powder

Filling
2 tamarillos
8 sheets gelatin
3 tablespoons orange liqueur
1 cup confectioners' sugar
2 cups heavy cream
2 teaspoons vanilla sugar (see page 10) or a few drops vanilla extract

Topping
2 tamarillos
3½ oz quince jelly

Note
If you can't find tamarillos, use ripe persimmons or papaya instead.

1 Preheat the oven to 350°F. Grease a 9½-inch round springform pan.

2 Put the egg whites into a bowl with the salt and beat until they hold stiff peaks. Beat the egg yolks with the water and sugar until the sugar has dissolved. Mix the flour with the cornstarch and cocoa powder and loosely fold into the egg yolk mixture with the egg whites.

3 Spoon the batter into the prepared pan. Bake in the preheated oven for 50 minutes, then turn out onto a wire rack and let cool.

4 To make the filling, peel the tamarillos with a vegetable peeler, remove the stems, and puree the fruit using an immersion blender. Soak the gelatin in cold water for about 10 minutes, then squeeze out and place in a small saucepan with the liqueur and heat over low heat until dissolved. Mix with the tamarillo puree and confectioners' sugar.

5 Whip the cream with the vanilla sugar until it holds stiff peaks. Fold the tamarillo mixture into the cream.

6 Halve the sponge horizontally. Replace the bottom half in the pan and spread the tamarillo cream on top. Place the other half on top, cover the pan with plastic wrap, and let set in the refrigerator for about 4 hours.

7 To make the topping, peel the tamarillos with a vegetable peeler, remove the stems, and cut the fruit into thin slices with a sharp knife. Arrange the slices on the cake in a circular pattern. Put the gelatin into a small saucepan and heat over low heat, then brush it over the tamarillo slices.

Index